NATURE WATCH

JAGUARS

Written by
Sally M. Walker

Lerner Publications Company • Minneapolis

CONTENTS

For my friend Ben Austin and his pal Zak, a jaguar at heart

Text copyright © 2009 by Sally M. Walker
Map and diagram copyright © 2009 Independent Picture Service

Lerner Publications Company
A division of Lerner Publishing Group, Inc.
241 First Avenue North
Minneapolis, MN 55401 U.S.A.

Website address: www.lernerbooks.com

Library of Congress Cataloging-in-Publication Data

Walker, Sally M.
  Jaguars / by Sally M. Walker.
    p. cm. — (Nature watch)
  Includes bibliographical references and index.
  ISBN 978–0–8225–7510–8 (lib. bdg. : alk. paper)
  1. Jaguar—Juvenile literature. I. Title.
QL737.C23W32 2009
599.75'5—dc22   2007025965

Manufactured in the United States of America
1 2 3 4 5 6 – DP – 14 13 12 11 10 09

A jaguar on the move

SILENT STALKERS

DRY LEAVES RUSTLE BENEATH AN ARMADILLO'S SHUFFLING feet. Spots of sunlight gleam on its armor-covered body. Except for the armadillo, the forest undergrowth seems deserted. But it isn't. A large cat silently waits nearby. Its coat blends perfectly with the forest plants, making the cat almost invisible. The motionless cat watches the armadillo waddle across the forest floor. Suddenly, the cat leaps forward. Its paw swipes the armadillo off its feet. The cat's massive jaws clamp shut on the armadillo's body. Within seconds, the jaguar has grabbed the armadillo in its teeth and vanished into the thick forest undergrowth.

Studying an animal as quick and mysterious as the jaguar is a challenge for scientists. One way they have learned about jaguars is by studying their fossils. Fossils are the ancient remains of animals and plants

This crouching jaguar bowl is from Mexico. It was used for religious events.

The oldest jaguar fossils in North America are one and a half million years old. European and Asian jaguar fossils are even older. The oldest jaguar fossils have been found in Europe and Asia. Scientists believe that jaguars first came from those areas. They think jaguars may have **evolved**, or gradually changed, from leopard ancestors. These ancient jaguars were larger than today's jaguars.

About one and a half million years ago, some of these jaguars arrived in North America. They traveled across a stretch of land called the Bering Land Bridge, which used to connect Alaska and Asia. Then, thousands of years ago, ocean waters completely flooded the Bering Land Bridge. Jaguars could no longer travel from Asia to North America. Sometime after the land bridge flooded, all the jaguars in Europe and Asia became **extinct**, or died out. Since then, jaguars have lived only in North America, Central America, and South America.

Kings and noblemen from ancient American cultures are often pictured wearing a jaguar skin as a sign of their important place in society. Artwork containing jaguars appears on ancient buildings, in stone relief murals, in pottery shapes, and as jade artifacts.

A stone two-headed jaguar throne *(bottom)* is in the courtyard in front of the Governor's Palace in Uxmal, Mexico, an ancient Maya city.

The jaguar is the strongest **predator**, or animal that kills other animals for its food, in the areas where it lives. This may be one reason why, hundreds of years ago, the Aztec people in Mexico, the Maya in southern Mexico and Central America, and the Olmec in South America regarded the jaguar with awe. They treated it as a god. They believed the Jaguar God lived in the underworld and controlled the rain and lightning. The Olmec and Maya called it the Lord of the Night. Perhaps the jaguar's seemingly magical ability to vanish quickly into the forest gave it this name.

Most people no longer believe that the jaguar has supernatural abilities. But it is still regarded with awe. Scientists don't know as much about jaguars as they do about lions or tigers. Many are eager to learn more about this mysterious cat.

THE JAGUAR'S FAMILY TREE

Scientists classify, or sort, animals into groups according to features they share. Jaguars are members of a class, or large group of animals, called Mammalia. Animals in this class are called mammals. All mammals have at least some hair on their bodies, and a female mammal feeds her young with milk she produces in her body.

Jaguars belong to a family, or slightly smaller group of animals that share many features. The jaguar family is called Felidae. Members of this family are called felids. All cats are felids. They all have sharp teeth and are meat eaters.

The ocelot *(left)* and the bobcat *(below)* are other members of the family Felidae. Like the jaguar, they also live in the Americas. But they are smaller.

Lions are closely related to jaguars.

The name *jaguar* comes from the Tupi-Guaraní language that used to be spoken in areas of South America. The word *yaguara* referred to large meat eaters, including jaguars and other big cats. Modern people throughout Mexico, Central America, and South America often call the jaguar *el tigre* in Spanish, relating this fierce cat to its cousin, the tiger.

Scientists further classify animals into even smaller groups. Animals within a **genus** are even more alike than those grouped in a family. Jaguars belong to the genus *Panthera*. Lions, tigers, leopards, and snow leopards also belong to the genus *Panthera*.

The **species** is an even smaller classification group. Animals that are the same species are the most alike of all. They are able to breed, or produce young, with each other. Jaguars belong to the species *Panthera onca*. Jaguars that live in separate regions may have slightly different features. But they all belong to the same species.

WHERE JAGUARS ROAM

Jaguars used to live in many areas of the United States. By 1900, jaguars had become rare. Occasionally a jaguar strays from Mexico over the southern U.S. border and is seen in Texas or Arizona. But the United States has not had any breeding populations of jaguars since the early 1900s. Jaguars live only in parts of Mexico, Central America, and South America.

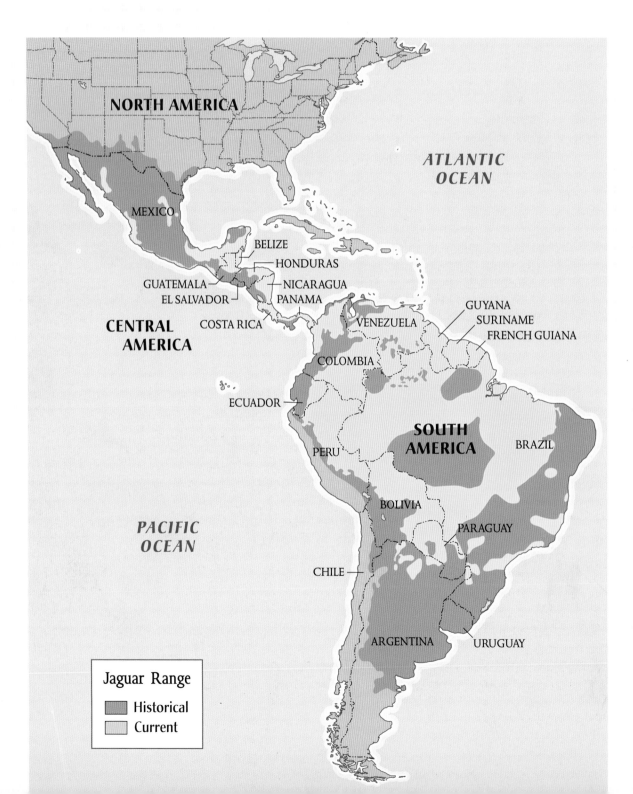

Jaguars live in tropical climates, which are warm year-round. They also live in temperate regions, where seasons change and become cooler during winter months. But they don't live high up on South American mountains, where it gets very cold in the winter.

Jaguars prefer to live in forests—moist lowland forests as well as drier temperate forests. Shrubs and trees give a jaguar plenty of places to hide and wait for **prey.** In tropical areas, tangled mangrove tree roots provide shelter. On the flat plains along rivers, large-leafed plants shield jaguars from the hot sun.

Jaguars also like rocky places that border grasslands or forests. Rocky ledges, cracks, and caves provide safe places to raise young. From there, jaguars wander through marshes, swamps, and grassy fields. Prey, or animals that jaguars eat, are plentiful in those places.

Jaguars are good swimmers, so they often live near a river or a lake. They frequently hop into the water for a quick swim on a hot day. People who have trapped jaguars have reported that many were missing the tips of their tails. Piranhas, meat-eating fish found in South American waters, had bitten them off!

A jaguar takes a swim.

PHYSICAL CHARACTERISTICS

PREHISTORIC JAGUARS HAD LONGER LEGS AND LARGER BODIES than modern jaguars. Over tens of thousands of years, the legs have shortened and the jaguar's body has become smaller and stockier. Even so, the jaguar is the largest cat that lives in Mexico, Central America, or South America.

Male jaguars usually weigh up to 265 pounds (120 kg), and they may grow up to 6 feet (2 m) long. The tail adds another 1.5 to 2.5 feet (0.5–0.8 m). Female jaguars are smaller. They usually weigh up to 200 pounds (90 kg) and grow up to 5.4 feet (1.6 m) in body length.

Jaguars are much stockier than other large cats, such as lions and tigers. Scientists believe jaguars' shorter, chunkier bodies help make them more efficient hunters in the shrub-filled areas where they live. They can hide more easily in low brush (*above*) than lions or tigers could.

The color and pattern of the jaguar's fur also help jaguars to be successful predators. The coat, or fur, on most jaguars' backs and sides is orange or dark yellow. It has black spots arranged in patterns called rosettes. Each rosette is formed by a circle of black dots with one or more black dots inside it. Rosettes may be small or large. Looking at the rosette pattern is a good way to tell jaguars from leopards. A leopard does not have extra dots in the center of its rosettes.

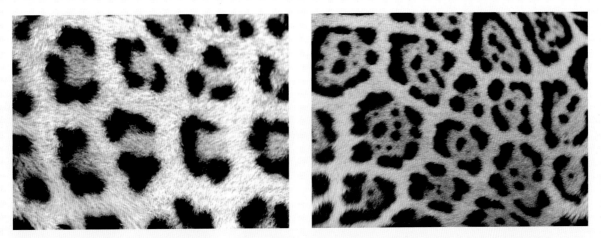

Which picture shows the jaguar spots? Which side has the leopard spots? The answer is on page 45.

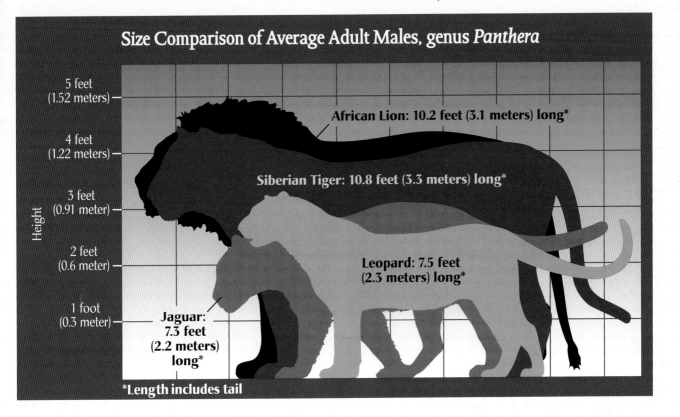

Size Comparison of Average Adult Males, genus *Panthera*

5 feet (1.52 meters) —
4 feet (1.22 meters) —
3 feet (0.91 meter) —
2 feet (0.6 meter) —
1 foot (0.3 meter) —

Height

African Lion: 10.2 feet (3.1 meters) long*

Siberian Tiger: 10.8 feet (3.3 meters) long*

Leopard: 7.5 feet (2.3 meters) long*

Jaguar: 7.3 feet (2.2 meters) long*

***Length includes tail**

13

This black jaguar is from Brazil. Its rosettes are visible in bright sunlight.

When a jaguar hides in shrubs or among other forest plants, its coat **camouflages** it perfectly. The black rosettes and the orange background look just like a mix of sun dapples and the shadows cast by leaves. On a jaguar's chin, throat, belly, and the inner part of its legs, the coat fades to a white or cream color. This light-colored fur also has black spots.

A small number of jaguars are completely black. A jaguar's coloring is passed down from its parents. Scientists have noticed that black jaguars are more common in areas where the temperatures are very high and the air is very humid. Even though the fur appears to be totally black, traces of a darker rosette pattern are still visible in strong sunlight.

The jaguar's head, like the rest of its body, is chunkier than the heads of other large wild cats. That's because the jaguar's jaw muscles are very well developed. Strong jaws are necessary for its diet. They must be able to crack hard materials such as bones.

Jaguars have keen eyesight and are very good at judging distances. This lets them leap and expertly pounce on their prey. Like people, jaguars have binocular vision. Their eyes move together and form one image. That way they can accurately zero in on objects in their field of vision. (Many birds, on the other hand, have eyes that move separately. That lets them see more of their surroundings at once.)

A jaguar's strong jaws are good for biting and tearing meat.

The jaguar has long, pointed ears. They are made up of a soft, flexible tissue called cartilage. The top portion of a person's ear is also made of cartilage. A jaguar's ears are sensitive enough to pick up even the quietest rustling sounds made by small prey scurrying through the brush. Muscles at the base of each ear allow a jaguar's ears to swivel in the direction of a sound. Moving its ears helps a jaguar pinpoint its prey's location.

Jaguars have a good sense of smell. They use this sense mostly to determine the whereabouts of other jaguars. When they hunt, jaguars rely more on their eyesight and hearing to locate prey.

All jaguars rely on their **vibrissae**, or whiskers, to supply them with information about their surroundings. Vibrissae are found in several places on the jaguar's head. Most vibrissae are on either side of the jaguar's upper lip. Several are just above the cat's eyes, where people have eyebrows. Vibrissae also stick out along the sides of the jaguar's head.

A jaguar's ears do not have to turn together in the same direction.

A jaguar's vibrissae are sensitive to touch and motion.

Vibrissae are wider at the base than they are at the tip. The skin at the base of each of the vibrissae contains many nerves that are sensitive to touch and motion. When the cat is resting, the vibrissae on its upper lip jut out to each side. They shift a little bit forward when the jaguar is walking. If the cat roams among narrowly spaced shrubs or trees, its vibrissae may brush against them. When vibrissae on both sides are brushed, the jaguar knows the space may be too narrow for its body to squeeze through.

17

Left: A jaguar's short legs are muscular.
Below: Each front paw has five toes. Four face forward and touch the ground.

Vibrissae are also important when a jaguar is capturing prey. Then the whiskers jut out in front of the cat's mouth, especially when the cat bites into its prey. Scientists believe that when the vibrissae are in this position, the nerves at their bases send a lightning-quick message to the jaguar's brain. They sense the prey's position and become like arrows pointing directly at the spot where the jaguar needs to bite hard to prevent its prey from escaping.

The jaguar's body is designed to hunt and survive. Its stocky legs are well suited for pouncing and leaping. Muscles in a jaguar's short front legs cushion its body when the cat leaps and lands on prey. The front paws are powerful enough to swipe even large prey off its feet. A jaguar's muscular front paws help it climb up tree trunks too.

Each of a jaguar's front paws has five toes. Back paws have only four toes. Inside each paw, bands of tissue called ligaments bind the toe bones tightly together so they can support the jaguar's body as it leaps and lands.

Each toe ends in a sharp claw made of **keratin**, the same substance that forms human fingernails and toenails. Like a housecat, a jaguar can retract its claws, or pull them in so they don't stick out. Jaguars contract, or squeeze, their toe ligaments to extend the claws. The long, hook-shaped claws are very effective at stabbing prey.

The fifth claw on each front paw is called the dewclaw. It is located on the inside of the leg, a short distance higher than the other toes. Dewclaws do not touch the ground when cats walk. A jaguar uses its dewclaws when it wraps its front paws around prey. Like a thumb, a dewclaw gives the jaguar extra grasping ability, especially when the claw's sharp point digs in.

Pads on the underside of each paw cushion the jaguar's legs as it runs and pounces. The soft pads also enable the jaguar to move silently across the forest floor. Jaguars can move so quietly that people often do not realize a jaguar has passed nearby until they find its tracks, called **pugmarks**.

Above: **A jaguar's paws have thick pads.** *Inset:* **Pugmarks show that a jaguar walked here.**

19

LIFE
CYCLE

JAGUARS LIVE ALONE MOST OF THE TIME. BUT THEY DO approach one another when they are ready to breed. A male jaguar is mature and ready to breed when he is three to four years old. A female can have her first litter, or group of babies, when she is two to three years old. After mating, the male and female do not stay together as a pair.

In zoos, jaguars breed and give birth year-round. In the wild, jaguars in tropical areas may also breed year-round. They only need a steady food supply and conditions favorable to newborn cubs. But jaguars that live in temperate climates, such as in the Pantanal wetland in Brazil, have breeding seasons. The exact months of the breeding season vary from place to place, according to the climate. Cubs must be born at a time when food is plentiful for them and the nursing mother.

Gestation is the period of time in which a baby grows inside its mother. It lasts 91 to 111 days for jaguars. When a female is ready to give birth, she seeks a safe hiding place. This may be a rocky den or a thick stand of plants. Jaguars give birth to one to four cubs in each litter.

Most frequently, a litter contains two cubs. A litter of one or three is less common. A litter of four cubs is rare.

A female jaguar is very protective of her cubs and of the place where she gives birth. She drives away any jaguars that stray near the den or her cubs.

Above: A female jaguar lies with her cub in their rocky den. The cub is four days old.
Opposite: A pair of jaguars playfully get ready to mate.

A newborn cub is completely dependent on its mother. Its eyes are sealed shut and will not open until the cub is three days to two weeks old. The cub is a pale yellow color, with black spots on its back and sides. It has stripes on its face. The yellow coloring deepens as the cub grows.

At birth, a cub is only about 16 inches (40 cm) long and weighs about 30 ounces (850 g). But it gains weight rapidly as it nurses on its mother's rich milk. The cub will continue nursing until it is five to six months old. However, it won't wait that long before it starts eating meat. A cub usually gets its first taste of meat when it is about two weeks old.

A jaguar cub eats a spotted paca. The cub's mother killed this rodent. But the cub defends it fiercely.

Above: **A jaguar gives her four-week-old cub a bath.** *Inset:* **A cub calls for its mother.**

When a cub is about 18 days old, it starts to walk around and explore its den and the area nearby. The mother jaguar stays close by. She keeps a sharp eye out for animals that might harm the cub. Sometimes, though, a cub wanders out of sight. Then it calls for its mother.

Very young cubs cannot mew. Instead, they make a sound that scientists describe as a bleat. It sounds a little like the sound a sheep makes. The bleat changes into a mew when the cub is three to six months old. By the time a cub turns one year old, it makes all of the sounds an adult jaguar can make.

An older cub and its mother rest beside a rain forest pond.

The female jaguar cares for her cubs until they are one and a half to two years old. During that time, she teaches them how to hunt so they can survive on their own. After a cub leaves its mother, it may return once or twice to the area where it was born and stay for a couple of months. After that, it leaves the area permanently. By then, the mother is ready to breed again. Female jaguars can have a litter about every two years.

The siblings may stay together as a hunting pair for a few months after they first leave their mother. Eventually, though, they separate and each establishes its own **home range**, the area where it will live and breed. Male cubs usually roam farther away from the area where they were born than female cubs do.

The life span of jaguars varies greatly, depending on their environment. In the wild, jaguars seldom live longer than 10 or 11 years. Hunters or disease often kill them. In zoos, however, jaguars can live 20 to 25 years.

Jaguar siblings form a special bond growing up together as cubs. They may continue to live and hunt together for a while after leaving their mother.

DAILY ROUTINE AND DIET

SCIENTISTS HAVE LEARNED MUCH ABOUT JAGUARS BY studying captive animals in zoos. But to learn how they hunt and behave in the wild, scientists must observe jaguars in their natural **habitat**, the place where they normally live and raise young. However, observing jaguars isn't easy. They are difficult to track because they are so good at slipping quickly and silently through the undergrowth.

Radio telemetry is a useful tool for keeping tabs on a jaguar. To monitor jaguars this way, scientists first have to catch one. Sometimes dogs are used to track a jaguar. The dogs follow the scent trail of a jaguar until the cat is sighted. A jaguar is powerful enough to kill a dog, but it flees

Dogs chase the fleeing jaguar until it climbs into a tree. Then scientists shoot the jaguar with a tranquilizer dart. This makes the jaguar sleepy and unable to move around. The drugs used to quiet the jaguar are carefully chosen and given in accurately measured doses so they do not permanently harm the animal.

A jaguar may also be caught in a cage or wooden box. Live bait, such as a pig or goat, is placed inside the cage. A hungry jaguar enters the cage to catch its prey. Once the cat is inside the cage, the door shuts, and the cat is tranquilized with a dart.

Once caught, the drugged jaguar is measured and weighed. Usually the cat is given an antibiotic, a medicine that controls infection. Scientists do this so the small wound made by the dart will not become infected. The animal's teeth are examined and its body is checked for overall health.

Right: A researcher checks the teeth of a jaguar while it is drugged.
Below: Researchers from the National University of Costa Rica set this live trap for jaguars. They are studying jaguars in Costa Rica's Corcovado National Park.
Opposite: A drugged jaguar is wearing a radio collar. Its dangerous jaws are tied shut. This will protect the scientists if the jaguar wakes up too soon.

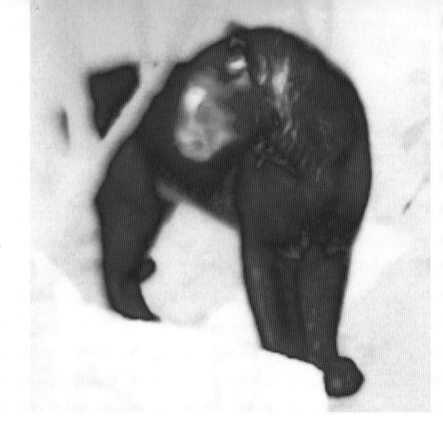

This scientific image is called a thermograph. It shows temperatures on this jaguar's body. Orange and yellow colors in its jaw may mean it has fever or swelling in that area. This jaguar may have a toothache.

Usually scientists take a small sample of the jaguar's blood. It will be sent to a laboratory where it can be studied. Scientists can learn about the jaguar's health by studying certain substances contained it its blood. They will look for tiny creatures called parasites that may live inside the jaguar's body. They will also check to see what kinds of bacteria and viruses might be in the jaguar's system. These all affect the cat's overall health.

In addition, scientists often take a sample of the jaguar's hair or even a small sample of body tissue. These are used to study the jaguar's DNA, the genetic material found inside every animal's cells. By studying jaguar DNA, scientists can determine how jaguars in different areas may be related to one another.

After the jaguar's body is measured and samples collected, a special collar containing a radio transmitter is fastened around the jaguar's neck. The transmitter sends out a radio signal that is detected by special receivers. Scientists fasten the receivers in trees or on a mountaintop in areas where the jaguar is known to go. Once the cat has been released, scientists can use the radio signals to track it.

Sometimes a small plane carries a receiver inside it. Scientists riding in the plane can follow a collared jaguar as it wanders to different parts of its home range.

Home on the Range

The size of a jaguar's home range varies according to place, sex, and season. In Brazil, in South America, a male jaguar's territory is 19 to 29 square miles (50–76 sq. km). In Belize, in Central America, a male's home range is about half that size. A male's home range is usually about twice the size of a female's.

During rainy seasons, flooding lakes and rivers may force a jaguar to live on a smaller home range if water covers part of its home. In a dry season or drought, a jaguar may have to extend its home range. It may have to roam farther to find prey that have left the area in search of water or food.

A jaguar spends at least one-third of its time sleeping or resting in thickets or among rocks that provide enough coverage to hide it when it lies flat. Jaguars often rest during the daytime. Jaguars are active at dusk and during the night. That's when they regularly wander around their home ranges. As they roam, they mark the boundary of their home ranges in several ways.

A black jaguar relaxes in a tree.

Jaguars regularly scratch on tree trunks, as house cats do on scratching posts. Scientists think the scratch marks may serve as a warning to other jaguars that they are entering "private property." Scratching also cleans the claws. Sometimes a jaguar uses its hind feet to make scrape marks in the soil. These marks also may let other jaguars know they are straying into occupied territory.

If a jaguar urinates on top of soil it has scraped loose, it sends an extra-strong message to keep out. Scent-marking the ground, trees, and rocks with urine or feces (solid body waste) is an effective way for a jaguar to make its presence known to others.

Jaguars have other ways to mark their scent too. Like other cats, a jaguar has scent glands on its head. House cats rub their heads on furniture, and even on people, to mark them as theirs. Similarly, when a jaguar rubs its head against a tree, its scent is left behind, marking that place as its home.

A jaguar claws a slim tree trunk. Its scratching leaves marks on the tree.

Two adult jaguars are ready to fight.

KEEPING TO THEMSELVES

Small parts of male jaguars' home ranges sometimes overlap. And a female's home range often overlaps the ranges of several males. It may also overlap those of other females. However, both males and females are careful to avoid meeting other jaguars, especially when females have cubs.

Sniffing out scent trails is one of the ways jaguars avoid encountering one another. A jaguar may stay in one small area of its home range for several days. But then it wanders around, sniffing trees and bushes for scent markings made by other jaguars. Male jaguars leave scent trails as they patrol the boundaries of their home ranges. A scent trail is a warning to other males that the area is occupied. A fresh scent trail means another jaguar is in the area. A faded scent trail means an encounter is unlikely because the other cat has moved on.

Jaguars also use **vocalization** to avoid encountering each other. By calling out, a jaguar tells nearby cats that it is there. Jaguars do not roar like lions do. Instead, a jaguar makes a series of five or more hoarse coughing sounds. The noise has been described as the sound you might make if you coughed deep in your throat while saying "uh, uh, uh, uh, uh." The coughing sound gets faster and louder until it can be heard from a distance. The jaguar repeats the series of coughs several times. Males also use vocal calls to attract females during breeding season. Adult males call in a deeper tone than females.

Sometimes males patrolling the boundaries of their home ranges do encounter one another. If growls don't frighten off one of the cats, a fight may occur. But fights are rare and are seldom fatal. The dominant male, the one that is stronger and usually older, drives off the younger male.

HUNTING

At night, jaguars do more than patrol their home ranges. They also hunt. A jaguar has good night vision. The **pupil**, or the black center part, of a jaguar's eye is a thin slit in daylight. At night, the pupil becomes large and round to let in more light. The retina, an area in the back of the eye, senses light. Behind a jaguar's retina is a layer of cells called the **tapetum**. The tapetum reflects light back through the retina, so the retina see the light two times instead of one. This means better vision in the dark. This gives the cat a hunting advantage as it stalks prey at night.

Jaguars are meat eaters. They do not supplement their diets with plants. They must hunt down and capture prey to get food. A jaguar hunts in several ways. The cat may hide and wait motionlessly until its prey is within reach, then spring out quickly in a deadly ambush. A jaguar may also stalk its prey silently for a short distance. When the time is right, a few large leaps powered by its muscular haunches land the cat on top of its prey.

Some large cats kill prey by biting it on the throat or on the nose. Jaguars seldom do this. A jaguar brings down its prey with a quick bite to the back of the skull or neck. The jaguar's massive jaws crush the bone. Its teeth damage the prey's brain and nerves. That leaves the prey unable to move.

A jaguar sinks its teeth into a white-tipped peccary. The jaguar's bone-crushing bite to the back of the peccary's neck kills it quickly.

A jaguar's strong teeth can crush toenails, hooves, bones—even turtle shells. Jaguars that eat turtles are skilled at using their front paws too. Sometimes, instead of crushing a turtle's shell with its teeth, a jaguar will use its paws to scoop out the flesh. The completely intact shell is all that is left behind.

A jaguar bites into a turtle.

When attacking large prey, such as deer or cattle, a jaguar jumps onto the animal's side or back. One wide front paw hooks over the animal's head, twisting it around. This causes the animal to fall. Often the fall breaks the animal's neck.

Some jaguars seem to prefer certain kinds of prey. But jaguars are opportunistic hunters—they will catch and eat any prey that they can. Depending on where a jaguar lives, it hunts animals such as capybaras (large rodents), peccaries (animals similar to pigs), armadillos, freshwater turtles, caimans (similar to alligators), fish, deer, monkeys, and wading birds.

A young jaguar catches a fish.

33

A jaguar has a well-designed set of teeth.

A hungry jaguar may also kill horses, pigs, and cattle. Livestock are easy prey because the animals live in large groups in open areas with no hiding places. Young horses and cattle are especially easy food for jaguars, because they are weaker than mature animals and less likely to escape. Scientists have found that once a jaguar has preyed on livestock, it often returns to kill more. And if a jaguar cub grows up eating livestock, when it grows up and has young of its own, they will be more likely to prey on livestock too.

When a jaguar kills large prey in an open area, it usually drags the prey to a hidden spot. The cat's strong **canines**, or fanglike front teeth, stab and hold the prey's body as it is being dragged. Once the cat has privacy, it uses its **incisors**, the smaller teeth between the canines, to pull feathers or fur from prey. Then its canines and incisors rip meat from the bones. The large, thin premolars and **molars** at the back of a jaguar's mouth are its slicing teeth. The cat shifts meat to the side of its mouth so these teeth can cut into the flesh. Jaguars may eat the complete carcass—bones, hooves, and all. Scientists know this because they have found feces that contain them.

Like other cats, jaguars have **papillae**, or small spinelike structures, on their tongues. Papillae make the tongue work like a file. When a jaguar licks a carcass, the papillae scrape away small bits of meat that cling to the bone. After eating a meal, a jaguar licks itself clean. Then the papillae comb through the jaguar's fur.

After a jaguar kills and eats large prey, such as a peccary or capybara, it does not need to eat again for about three days. If the prey was small, the jaguar may eat sooner.

The jaguar plays an important role as the largest predator in its **ecosystem**. An ecosystem is the community of plants and animals in an area. Jaguars help maintain the balance of their ecosystem. They help keep the ecosystem healthy by controlling the populations of their prey. When jaguars are no longer present in the ecosystem, the prey animals increase in number. That hurts other parts of the ecosystem. As the population of plant eaters grows, the animals eat more plants. Many animals may starve if most of an area's plants are eaten. A healthy ecosystem depends on having many different kinds of plants and animals living in it. The well-being of the ecosystem can be threatened if jaguars are removed.

A jaguar yawns, showing off its long tongue.

JAGUARS AND THE FUTURE

JAGUARS ARE IN DANGER OF BECOMING EXTINCT. PEOPLE are one of the main reasons why jaguars are **endangered**.

People are the only animals capable of preying on adult jaguars. People have hunted and killed jaguars for many years and for several reasons. Often, farmers and ranchers kill a jaguar because it killed their livestock. When jaguars kill livestock, farmers and ranchers lose money. So they hunt the jaguar they think is responsible for the killing—or hire hunters to do so. Unfortunately, the jaguar that is killed isn't always the one that ate the livestock.

Surprisingly, attempts to kill a jaguar that preys on livestock may actually cause more livestock deaths. That's because hunters often only wound the jaguar they are tracking. If a bullet badly damages a jaguar's leg or breaks its teeth, the cat may be unable to catch its normal prey. It must turn toward easy prey, such as livestock, in order to survive.

Sport hunters have killed jaguars for trophies and for their skin. Uncontrolled hunting of jaguars in the past is a major reason why jaguars no longer live in the United States. In 1972, the U.S. Fish and Wildlife Service classified jaguars as endangered. They are still officially an endangered species.

Jaguar skins used to be in huge demand for the fur coat fashion market. Scientists estimate that during the late 1960s, as many as 15,000 jaguars per year were killed in Brazil for their fur. Many thousands more were killed in Mexico, Central America, and South America. The furs were sold around the world. In 1973, jaguars were listed in Appendix I of the Convention on International Trade in Endangered Species (CITES). This made it against the law in most countries to hunt and kill jaguars for commercial purposes, including fur trading. But **poachers**, or people who hunt illegally, are still a danger to jaguars.

The Convention on International Trade in Endangered Species (CITES) is an agreement among countries. Governments monitor the international trade of wild plants and animals, and they protect certain species. Species listed in Appendix I, such as jaguars, are in danger of becoming extinct. They may not be traded except in rare cases. Species listed in Appendix II or Appendix III may be traded internationally, but the trade is controlled. More than 170 countries have joined CITES.

Poachers in Brazil skin a jaguar.

After hunters, habitat loss is the other main threat to jaguars. In some areas, trees are cut down to make products such as furniture or paper. In other places, trees are cut to make room for fields. The fields are planted with crops or turned into pastureland for livestock. To reach these areas, people build roads. The roads make it easier for more people to spread into jaguar habitats and build homes. People have moved into many of the areas where jaguars live.

Prey in the jaguars' habitat also lose their homes and lives when people move in. With less prey around, jaguars are more likely to hunt livestock for their meals. And that, in turn, angers ranchers. So what can be done?

First, scientists are working with ranchers to help solve the problem of jaguars preying on livestock. In some places, electric fences have been an effective solution. When a jaguar attempts to pass through an electric fence, it receives a painful shock. The shock is strong enough to make the jaguar stop, but not strong enough to permanently harm or kill it.

Left: A road cuts through a rain forest in Guatemala. Traffic brings noise and air pollution to jaguars' habitats. *Below:* Boats are a danger to swimming jaguars. People have built homes and docks for their boats on this river in Brazil.

Jaguars prefer wooded or rocky terrain. Cattle kept near such areas in Central and South America may become jaguar prey.

Scientists suggest that farmers keep very young or very old livestock away from areas where jaguars are likely to roam, such as fields near forested areas. Those animals are the easiest for jaguars to prey upon. If possible, livestock-killing jaguars could be captured and moved to a new area far from ranches and farms. If money is available, ranchers and farmers could be repaid for the value of their livestock killed by jaguars.

Scientists also suggest that people hunt fewer jaguar prey animals for their own food. In some areas of Brazil, people and jaguars hunt some of the same animals, such as capybaras and peccaries, for food. People could turn to available alternative foods, leaving more prey for jaguars.

Above: A river cuts through a rain forest in Belize.
Right: Dr. Alan Rabinowitz was honored in
2004 for his work for jaguars.

Some scientists suggest that conservationists, or people who act to preserve the environment, work with ranchers to patrol ranch lands. Organized groups would keep an eye out for jaguars and also for cattle rustlers, or people who steal cattle. Jaguars are blamed for many missing cattle, but sometimes rustlers are responsible for the losses.

Another way to protect jaguars is by establishing wildlife sanctuaries, or places where it is against the law to hunt. Game wardens or rangers patrol these areas regularly to make sure poachers stay out.

Some sanctuaries have already been created. In the early 1980s, scientist Alan Rabinowitz studied jaguars in the forested Cockscomb Basin of Belize in Central America. He realized how important it was to protect the shrinking jaguar population. He worked tirelessly with others until the area was declared a national forest reserve. Hunting jaguars is not allowed there. In 1986, the area became the Cockscomb Basin Wildlife Sanctuary. It was the world's first jaguar preserve.

Since then, other countries in Central America and South America have also set aside lands as reserves and sanctuaries. But scientists are realizing this isn't enough. Jaguars need to breed with jaguars from other areas. Inbreeding, or breeding among related animals, produces animals that may get sick more easily. Breeding among jaguars that are not related keeps a jaguar population healthy. So scientists suggest establishing narrow, protected, forested corridors to connect preserves. These corridors would let jaguars move safely from one preserve to another.

Educating people with facts about jaguars and their importance in the ecosystem is an important step in preventing the jaguar's extinction. Many people have mistaken ideas about jaguars, including the false belief that jaguars regularly hunt humans. Helping people understand these cats may raise interest in protecting them.

Tourists hike through a forest in Guatemala.

Because of the jaguar's fierceness and beauty, it is a perfect flagship species, or animal used to represent its endangered environment. The Belize Zoo uses the jaguar as a flagship species. Since 1983, zoo employees have worked hard to draw attention to the jaguar. Their work is paying off. As Belize's citizens have learned more about jaguars, they are becoming proud of the jaguar and its place in their country's natural heritage. They are more willing to help protect jaguars and preserve their habitat. In turn, this helps preserve the whole area because people from other regions and countries want to come and see jaguars. **Ecotourism**—people touring natural habitats in a way that won't harm plants or animals—is proving to be a very profitable business in some jaguar habitats. It provides money for local people without endangering jaguars or the environment.

The jaguar is one of the most fascinating and mysterious big cats. It has roamed the land for many thousands of years. If we take action now and are careful, we can ensure that jaguars will continue to roam in the future.

Above: A thirsty jaguar takes a drink in the Belize Zoo. *Opposite:* A jaguar grooms her cub.

GLOSSARY

camouflage: to hide an animal or thing by making it look like its surroundings (as a jaguar's coloring does)

canines: fanglike teeth on either side of the front biting teeth

ecosystem: the community of plants and animals in an area

ecotourism: people touring natural habitats in a way that won't harm the plants or animals within them

endangered: in danger of dying out

evolve: to change gradually over time

extinct: died out. A species with no more living members is extinct.

genus: a scientific grouping of animals that contains closely related species. Jaguars, lions, tigers, leopards, and snow leopards share the genus *Panthera.*

gestation: the period of time in which a baby grows inside its mother before it is born

habitat: the type of place in which an animal or plant normally lives

incisors: front teeth used to bite and rip meat or pull out fur or feathers

home range: the area in which a jaguar lives, hunts, and breeds

keratin: the protein substance that forms claws, fingernails, and hair

molars: large teeth at the back of the mouth. Together with premolars, the teeth in front of the molars, they slice through flesh as a jaguar chews.

papillae: small, spinelike structures on a cat's tongue

poachers: people who hunt animals illegally

predator: an animal that kills other animals for food

prey: an animal hunted by another animal for food

pugmarks: footprints left by a wild animal

pupil: the black center part of the eye. The pupil controls how much light enters the eye.

species: a group of animals that are related closely enough to breed with one another. Jaguars belong to the species *Panthera onca.*

tapetum: a layer of cells in the back of a jaguar's eye that reflects light back to the retina and lets the jaguar see better in the dark

vibrissae: stiff hairs that stick out from a jaguar's face and help it sense its surroundings

vocalization: calling out. Jaguars vocalize to announce their presence and ward off other jaguars. They also use vocalization to attract mates.

SELECTED BIBLIOGRAPHY

Brown, David E. *Borderland Jaguars*. Salt Lake City: University of Utah Press, 2001.

Conforti, Valéria A. "Local Perceptions of Jaguars (*Panthera onca*) and pumas (*Puma concolor*) in the Iguaçu National Park area, South Brazil." *Biological Conservation*, June 2003, 215–221.

Gilbert, Stephen G. *Pictorial Anatomy of the Cat*. Seattle, WA: University of Washington Press, 1968.

Hoogesteijn, Rafael, and Edgardo Mondolfi. *The Jaguar*. Caracas, Venezuela: Armitano, 1992.

Kitchener, Andrew. *The Natural History of the Wild Cats*. Ithaca, NY: Comstock Pub. Associates, 1991.

Medellín, R.A., et al. *El Jaguar en el Nuevo Milenio*. New York: Wildlife Conservation Society, 2002.

Miller, S. Douglas, and Daniel D. Everett, eds. *Cats of the World*. Washington, D.C.: National Wildlife Federation, 1986.

Novacek, Michael J., ed. *The Biodiversity Crisis*. New York: New Press, 2001.

Sanderson, Eric W., et al. "Planning to Save a Species: the Jaguar as a Model." *Conservation Biology*, February 2002, 58–72.

Turner, Alan. *The Big Cats and Their Fossil Relatives*. New York: Columbia University Press, 1997.

The answer for the question on page 13 is the jaguar rosettes are on the right. The leopard spots are on the left.

WEBSITES

Black Jaguar

http://www.sandiegozoo.org/kids/animal_profile_jaguar.html

Check out photos and a profile of Orson, the black jaguar that lives at the San Diego Zoo in California.

Jaguar

http://animals.nationalgeographic.com/animals/mammals/jaguar.html

Visit this National Geographic Society website to listen to a recording of jaguar sounds and follow links to learn about other wild cats.

Jaguars: Phantoms of the Night

http://www.nationalgeographic.com/ngm/0105/feature2/media.html

On this multimedia website, *National Geographic* photographer Steve Winter takes you through a slideshow based on his experience photographing jaguars in their natural habitat.

Save the Jaguar

http://www.savethejaguar.com

Learn more about these endangered cats, find out about recent research and conservation efforts, and catch up on jaguar news on this website by the Wildlife Conservation Society.

FURTHER READING

Johnston, Marianne. *Big Cats Past and Present*. New York: Powerkids Press, 2000.

Kahn, Jeremy. "On the Prowl." *Smithsonian*, November 2007, 85– 92.

Markle, Sandra. *Lions*. Minneapolis: Lerner Publications Company, 2005.

Savage, Stephen. *Animals of the Rainforest*. Austin, TX: Raintree Steck-Vaughn, 1997.

Stone, Lynn M. *Tigers*. Minneapolis: Lerner Publications Company, 2005.

Woods, Theresa. *Jaguars*. Chanhassen, MN: Child's World, 2001.

INDEX

ABOUT THE AUTHOR

Sally M. Walker is the author of many award-winning nonfiction books for young readers. She is the author of *Secrets of a Civil War Submarine: Solving the Mysteries of the* H.L. Hunley, which won the prestigious Sibert Award in 2006. When she isn't busy writing or doing research for books, Ms. Walker works as a children's literature consultant. She gives presentations at many reading conferences and has taught at Northern Illinois University. Her other books with Lerner include *Magnetism, Light, Sound,* and *Electricity.*

PHOTO ACKNOWLEDGEMENTS

The images in this book are used with the permission of: © Steve Winter/National Geographic/Getty Images, all backgrounds, pp. 1, 5, 6, 9, 12, 13 (right), 20, 26, 27 (top), 28, 33, 36, 37, 44–48; © Michael & Patricia Fogden/ Minden Pictures/Getty Images, pp. 2–3, © John Giustina/Getty Images, p. 4; © Nick Gordon/naturepl.com, pp. 5, 21, 22; © University of Essex/Art Directors, p. 6; © Macduff Everton/CORBIS, p. 7; © Gerry Lemmo, pp. 8 (top), 38 (top), 40 (top), 41; © Photodisc/Getty Images, pp. 8 (bottom), 9; © Laura Westlund/Independent Picture Service, pp. 10, 13; © A. Rouse/Peter Arnold, Inc., pp. 11, 30; © NHPA/Andy Rouse, p. 12; © age fotostock/SuperStock, p. 13 (left); © Fabio Colombini Medeiros/Animals Animals, p. 14; © Ben Olavo/Alamy, p. 15; © James Strachan/The Image Bank/Getty Images, p. 16; © Frans Lemmens/Iconica/Getty Images, p. 17; © DLILLC/Corbis, p. 18 (left); © Shattil & Rozinski/naturepl.com, p. 18 (right); © Theo Allofs/Visuals Unlimited, p. 19 (top); © Hans-Peter Moehlig/Alamy, p. 19 (bottom); © Tom Brakefield/CORBIS, pp. 20, 32; AP Photo/Thomas Haentzschel, p. 23 (left); © Tom Brakefield/ SuperStock, p. 23 (right); © James Beveridge/Visuals Unlimited, p. 24; © Mark Newman/SuperStock, p. 25; © Patricio Robles Gil/Oxford Scientific Films, p. 26; © Nick Turner/Minden Pictures, p. 27 (bottom); © Nutscode/T Service/ Photo Researchers, Inc., p. 28; © Anthony Mercieca/SuperStock, p. 29; © Luiz Claudio Marigo/naturepl.com, pp. 31, 36; © BIOS Bios-Auteurs (dro...)/Peter Arnold, Inc., p. 33 (top); © Gerard Lacz/Peter Arnold, Inc., p. 33 (bottom); © Carol Farneti Foster/ Oxford Scientific Films, p. 34; © John Gilbert Decd/Art Directors, p. 35; © A. Matos Dos Santos-UNEP/Peter Arnold, Inc, p. 37; © Jacques Jangoux/Visuals Unlimited, p. 38 (bottom); © Jane Sweeney/Art Directors, p. 39; © Zack Seckler/Getty Images, p. 40 (bottom); © Gerry Ellis/Minden Pictures/Getty Images, p. 42; © Peter Arnold, Inc./Alamy, p. 43.

Front cover: © Michael & Patricia Fogden/Minden Pictures/Getty Images

Back cover: © Steve Winter/National Geographic/Getty Images